IMAGES
of America

CLARINDA

This is one of many wonderful photographs of unidentified people housed with care at the Nodaway Valley Historical Museum. In this image, a lovely young Clarinda woman is showing off a typical party dress of the period between 1905 and 1910. (Courtesy of the Nodaway Valley Historical Museum Archives.)

ON THE COVER: In 1908, James and Thomas Martindale bought a business on the south side of the square. It was named Martindale Brothers Bakery, Restaurant & Confectionery Store. Later, they sold the business and each went into business for himself. James bought a bakery on the north side of the square. It was after the bakery burned that he bought a bakery on the west side. It was called Home Bakery & Café. This is where the south half of Taylor Pharmacy is now. In January 1938, James sold the business. (Courtesy of the Nodaway Valley Historical Museum Archives.)

IMAGES
of America
CLARINDA

Trish Okamoto

ARCADIA
PUBLISHING

Published by Arcadia Publishing
Charleston, South Carolina

Library of Congress Control Number: 2013947820

For all general information, please contact Arcadia Publishing:
Telephone 843-853-2070
Fax 843-853-0044
E-mail sales@arcadiapublishing.com
For customer service and orders:
Toll-Free 1-888-313-2665

Visit us on the Internet at www.arcadiapublishing.com

CONTENTS

ACKNOWLEDGMENTS

When it came time to compile and uncover documents, photographs, and stories, I came to realize that there really is no end to the telling of our wonderful history of Clarinda. With every discovery there is a new trail of three or four new avenues to research. With pleasure and a bit of determination, I am attempting to pursue each and every one of them. With this book I have included as much as I can about our heritage, being limited by pages, by using photographs to help all come to know and appreciate who came before us, and with that, how we arrived as well. This book could not be possible without my loving second home, the Nodaway Valley Historical Museum. Their amazing collection of documents and artifacts helped me every day I spent putting together this vast and amazing story of our community. But above all, I would like to thank one of our founding fathers, Elijah Miller, for his brilliance and foresight to record and document our beloved area via pen to let us share in his journey as he wandered with his son Webster Clark through the countryside of Page County. They studied and recorded every flower and every animal, and made many other observations during Clarinda's early development. Miller knew instinctively what people would need to prosper and grow, from the creation of a 16-block boulevard to the absolute need for trees to give Clarinda a healthy and appealing landscape, which he planned along with Dr. James Barrett. Many are fortunate to call this place home. We are forever grateful, Elijah Miller.

INTRODUCTION

Growing up in Clarinda, I had a certain childlike perspective of where I was living. I loved my library, school, and family, all of which were just a short bicycle trip away from any location in town. After 15 years of living in California as a woman, wife, and mother of two, my appreciation and my views have changed and become clearer. Living here now, I can truly say I cannot imagine living anywhere else. My family ties to this community go back to 1853, with my fourth great-grandfather Alexander Davis. He settled here along the banks of the river after a journey from Shelby County, Indiana. The love of our family history and heritage has brought me to a career that I love as the curator of the Nodaway Valley Historical Museum and guardian of all local history and genealogy. Writing this book is like telling the story of a great woman. A woman named Clarinda, who has sheltered and housed many. She has a rich story to tell, with some parts helping us realize how our community arrived where it is today. I feel honored, like so many, that she drew me into her story and allowed my family to become a part of her story for over 160 years.

Page County was surveyed in December 1845 and formally created in 1847. It was named for Capt. John Page, who was killed at the battle of Palo Alto during the Mexican War. The first two townships were surveyed under the direction of the surveyor general of Missouri. An error occurred in this work, and Missouri claimed a strip of Iowa land for some years after. This strip was about eight miles wide and ran through the second tier of townships. The reason for the mistake was that the survey commenced at the rapids on the Des Moines River instead of the Des Moines Rapids on the Mississippi, a difference of about nine miles. Both Missouri and Iowa petitioned Congress to settle the question, and a decision was made in favor of Iowa. In 1851, Page County's boundaries were finalized, measuring 23.75 miles east to west and 22.5 miles north to south. The county has a total area of 535 square miles, a small part of which is water. Under the leadership of William L. Burge, prosecuting attorney and acting judge, Clarinda was laid out in lots in May 1853. Elijah Miller was the surveyor, Benjamin Dodson was chairman, and Robert Stafford was axman. Many families over the past 160 years have been proud to call Clarinda and Page County home. Through these years, many have devoted their lives to the continued advancement of Clarinda as a community.

One

THE ARRIVAL

Although the 1850 census records around 500 people calling Page County home, credit for the development of the county seat of Clarinda must be given to a handful of determined men and their pioneer families. Clarinda was selected for the county seat in part because of a state act that was passed stating that the seat must be "as near the geographical center of the county as may be." In 1853, when Clarinda was platted, most of the population was located in the eastern part of the county. As the county grew, it became apparent that Clarinda was the best choice for a county seat. By 1853, Clarinda had become a center for business and education. The town was platted as a 49-block square around a public block. At this time, Clarinda was laid out to include a 100-foot-wide public area beginning two blocks out from the courthouse. This would later become the Promenade, or what is today called the Boulevard. This feature of Clarinda is still enjoyed today as an area for walking during the changing seasons. Clarinda has always taken much pride and control over its development. After the Civil War, when it was determined that the main line railroad would not be going through town, citizens took it upon themselves to build their own railroad connection. This pride and determination has continued over the past 160 years to help Clarinda develop into the place that many take pride in calling home.

This chapter is dedicated to all of those who came before and the amazing strength of character that they possessed. Residents owe so much to them, and this is a debt that can never truly be repaid, unless it is through their appreciation and support of this city. Locals continue to love and care for the community and watch it grow.

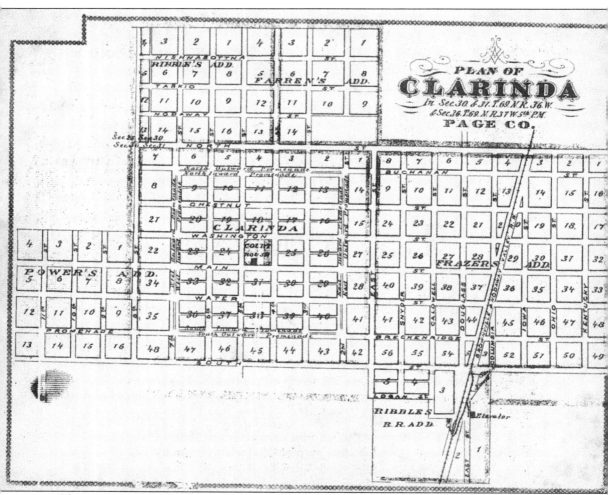

This map represents the dream that began Clarinda. Established in 1853, the layout has proved over time to be a thoughtful design. The town design would continue with additions to the 49-block square layout. (Courtesy of the Nodaway Valley Historical Museum Archives.)

Together with a handful of men, Elijah Miller surveyed and applied for the plat of Clarinda with the State of Iowa. The layout allowed for a town square for use as a courthouse or a park, a boulevard system to frame that two-block-square area, and an entire city block dedicated to a public school that all children could attend. Miller was an avid outdoorsman. He continued living in Clarinda until late in his life, when he moved to Mount Park, Oklahoma, to be close to his children. (Courtesy of the Nodaway Valley Historical Museum Archives.)

Clarinda is proud to call John R. Moreledge one of its first judges and founder. Moreledge, a lawyer, arrived in Clarinda from Indiana in 1857. After serving as county judge, he also served as mayor for a time. He worked along with Elijah Miller and other founding fathers to guarantee that Clarinda would succeed as county seat and become a community of which citizens could be proud. This photograph is the only known image of Moorledge, but his signature is prominent on many official documents during the early years of Clarinda. Born in England in 1812, he called Clarinda home for more than 25 years. After passing away in 1882, he was buried at the Clarinda Cemetery along with his wife and children. (Courtesy of the Nodaway Valley Historical Museum Archives.)

Robert Stafford arrived in Page County before Clarinda was established, in 1843. He is credited with being the first axman in Page County as well as being on the original recording of the first land purchase. He was elected to the position of sheriff in 1851. Working along with Elijah Miller and a handful of other settlers, he lived to see Page County prosper and helped develop this wonderful community. He passed away in 1879 at the age of 78 and is buried at the Clarinda Cemetery. (Courtesy of the Nodaway Valley Historical Museum Archives.)

THE UNITED STATES OF AMERICA,

To all to whom these presents shall come, greeting:

Pictured here is Robert Stafford's original land document, which is housed at the Nodaway Valley Historical Museum. The document was signed by Pres. Franklin Pierce and is dated June 15, 1855, granting founder Robert Stafford 40 acres of land in Page County on the eastern outskirts of Clarinda. Several of these original documents exist at the Nodaway Valley Historical Museum and record the government awarding land to men who applied for it and as payment for serving their country during times of war. (Courtesy of the Nodaway Valley Historical Museum Archives.)

Napoleon B. Moore was born in Ohio in 1832. After arriving in Clarinda in the 1850s, Moore established many businesses as well as a law practice. He became the county notary, took the county judgeship in 1861, and was elected a state senator, representing Page County from 1867 to 1871. His business sense brought about much success. At one point, Moore owned half the county in property. He was Page County and Clarinda's first millionaire. Moore called Clarinda home for over 50 years, but moved to Texas to be near family in 1900. He is buried there. (Courtesy of the Nodaway Valley Historical Museum Archives.)

Hon. N. B. MOORE,
Attorney at Law, Clarinda, Page Co.

The Stonebraker Mill was built in 1847 about two miles southeast of Clarinda. It served the growing county by furnishing sawed wood and cracked corn for the early settlers. Public meetings, court proceedings, and gatherings were held in the mill until the later buildings on the square could be built. The mill served families within a 40-mile radius. The mill was bought and sold to other pioneers over the next few years and known at one point as the Shambaugh Mill. In 1899, it burned to the ground and was never rebuilt. (Courtesy of the Nodaway Valley Historical Museum Archives.)

Once Clarinda began to develop, it drew many settlers and young couples during the 1850s and 1860s who were hoping for a home of their own and a community of which they could become a part. Joseph Davis arrived in Page County with his pioneer father, Alexander Davis, in the 1840s. Joseph returned to Ohio in 1860 so that he might marry and bring his 18-year-old childhood acquaintance Deborah Anna Latta to Clarinda to create a home and life of his own. (Courtesy of the Nodaway Valley Historical Museum Archives.)

Clarinda was platted and formed in 1853. This photograph from the late 1850s is thought to be one of the earliest images of the Clarinda Square. Notice the wooden sidewalk that protected citizens, especially the ladies with their full-length skirts, from the muddy street after a good shower. (Courtesy of the Nodaway Valley Historical Museum Archives.)

Two

WE WILL NEED A SQUARE

Many businesses came and went over the last 162 years in Clarinda, and most changed with the times. The original businesses were mercantile stores where citizens could purchase almost anything they needed at one location—from food to fabric or clothing. Later in the 1800s, specialty businesses offered products for more specific needs. But one thing remained: the need for a center of community, a place for business, shopping, and gathering. This chapter features a selection of Clarinda businesses that have been remembered and photographed. There are so many more men and women who conducted businesses over the years on the square, but images of these have never been found. Gradually, businesses moved out beyond the square location.

The Clarinda square was developed long before the courthouse finally came along in the 1870s. This first courthouse, which cost $7,456 to build, was used for about 10 years until the vault room within it proved to be inadequate, and the need was voiced to build a new courthouse. In 1885, the people approved construction of the new building at a cost of over $71,000.

These ladies are enjoying the afternoon and showing off some of the wonderful fashions of the 1920s. The east side of the square is the backdrop for this great photograph looking east from the courthouse courtyard. Notice the horse-drawn carriage in the background. This photograph was taken after the arrival of the automobile in Clarinda, yet many still preferred their horse-drawn conveyances. (Courtesy of the Nodaway Valley Historical Museum Archives.)

The Clement Furniture Store, shown here, was one of the first furniture makers to call Clarinda home. A.T. Clement (far left) created wonderful pieces and sold premade items. Standing on Clements's right is employee William Hutchings, who was not only known for his handiwork at Clement's but also as an undertaker, Methodist minister, and coffin maker. A.T. Clement built a wonderful home on South Fifteenth Street, and his work is still enjoyed today. (Courtesy of the Nodaway Valley Historical Museum Archives.)

Many businesses starting popping up around the square. The Boyers Jones Barber Shop was founded on the east side of the square. Despite the tight space, the business thrived for many years. This photograph was taken in 1902. (Courtesy of the Nodaway Valley Historical Museum Archives.)

Located on the east side of the square, Jones Drug offered many items to help with "whatever ailed you." Notice all of the glass jars. This photograph was taken around 1940, before the widespread use of plastic. (Courtesy of the Nodaway Valley Historical Museum Archives.)

This is a wonderful shot of the east side of the square taken around 1945. Notice in the far background the building advertising the Rialto Theatre. (Courtesy of the Nodaway Valley Historical Museum Archives.)

This photograph, taken around 1895, is the oldest image in existence of the east side of the square. The Regulator opened at that time and offered "on the Spot Cash" loans. Notice the crowning at the top of the building with the word "Crabill." Crabill Company was a well-known brick maker in Clarinda at that time and took much credit for the construction of some of the brick buildings on the square. It was common to call the east side of the square the Crabill Block. Sadly, this crowning is no longer present on the buildings. (Courtesy of the Nodaway Valley Historical Museum Archives.)

In 1907, four doors down on the east side of the square, one could find the Clarinda Music Conservatory, and next door, the Rural Phone Company. It was said that the sounds of both would compete. In the far background, the *Herald Journal* office on the corner of Fifteenth and Main Streets is visible. (Courtesy of the Nodaway Valley Historical Museum Archives.)

This view details the development of homes and businesses behind the east side of the square. Too bad only a handful of these old homes still exist today in Clarinda. (Courtesy of the Nodaway Valley Historical Museum Archives.)

This photograph was taken before 1902, when the curbs and paved streets were laid out. (Courtesy of the Nodaway Valley Historical Museum Archives.)

The C.P. Hewett Mercantile Company, pictured here in 1916, offered many items that women might need, from notions to bakeware and fashions. In 1916, the company closed its doors and held a public auction. An advertisement in the local paper stated that over $10,000 in inventory was being sold. (Courtesy of the Nodaway Valley Historical Museum Archives.)

This undated photograph is invaluable. It is known that J.H. Whitehill had a restaurant at this location along with the Ankeny Store and Bakery. Notice local dentist Dr. Harrison's office with the good doctor appearing in the north window. The Holcombe building was built by Lucinda H. Dearman Holcombe in 1905, a local woman of business; she also owned the millinery shop next door. (Courtesy of the Nodaway Valley Historical Museum Archives.)

The oldest-known photograph of the west side of the square was taken in 1867, long before the thought of paved streets. The ladies spoke of the seven inches of dirt on the bottom of their skirts after spending an afternoon on the square. The second building from the right is the law office of N.B. Moore, Page County's first millionaire. (Courtesy of the Nodaway Valley Historical Museum Archives.)

Many businesses in Clarinda, as well as other small towns, tried to drum up business by sending postcards depicting the local square. This one shows Clarinda's opera house on the corner as well as Weils Clothing store before it moved to its present location three doors down. (Courtesy of the Nodaway Valley Historical Museum Archives.)

This is a wonderful close-up shot of the west side of the square. In the distance, the Linderman Hotel is visible on the corner. (Courtesy of the Nodaway Valley Historical Museum Archives.)

Pictured here is the front of the Weils Clothing/Hawley Opera House. (Courtesy of the Nodaway Valley Historical Museum Archives.)

This photograph of the inside of Hawley's Store provides a visual testament to the vast amount of supplies available locally. Notice the fresh pineapples in the front. One wonders how many of those they sold in a week. (Courtesy of the Nodaway Valley Historical Museum Archives.)

Clarinda businesswoman Nancy Graff, along with her husband, Valentine, conducted business at the Graff Mercantile for many years. She is recorded as one of the first female business owners in Clarinda. Graff was also very well known for parading around town wearing all the new laces and textiles of the day, which were available for purchase at Graff Mercantile. She passed away in 1918 at the age of 71 and is laid to rest at the local Clarinda Cemetery. (Courtesy of the Nodaway Valley Historical Museum Archives.)

This photograph was taken in front of the Cramer Jewelry Store by the Benedict Piano company, which was upstairs above Cramer's, to advertise their massive sale (as it was called in the local paper). Their pianos, as well as the moving wagon for delivery, are on display. Note the instrument already loaded and ready. (Courtesy of the Nodaway Valley Historical Museum Archives.)

This photograph from the 1950s heralds the arrival of chain department stores along with mail-order service. In the distance, the Linderman Hotel is visible. (Courtesy of the Nodaway Valley Historical Museum Archives.)

This is one of the only full shots of the Page County Bank building, on the corner of today's Sixteenth and Washington Streets. This remained a bank for many years, then went through a few other businesses before being torn down. Today, a small green area exists in the spot. (Courtesy of the Nodaway Valley Historical Museum Archives.)

This photograph of one of Clarinda's earliest businesses was recently discovered by the Nodaway Valley Historical Museum. Brackens Book Store, Wall Paper and Toys was on the northeast corner of the square. Thomas Jefferson Bracken came to Page County on foot in 1854. He passed away in 1917 at the age of 85, one of Clarinda's most beloved citizens and businessmen. Mary A. Davison Bracken and their son are pictured here in front of the store. (Courtesy of the Nodaway Valley Historical Museum Archives.)

This is one of the earliest photographs of Clarinda, taken in 1866, just 13 years after the settlement was platted. The were not a lot of luxuries, judging by street conditions. After a hard winter, the ground was very cold and hard, which made it difficult for the horses. For the most part, only the gentlemen ventured out on these kinds of days. In the distance, the City Grocery Store and the Ribble Hotel are visible on the corner. The Ribble Hotel was established as the stagecoach stop in 1854, before the large brick buildings went up on the square. (Courtesy of the Nodaway Valley Historical Museum Archives.)

Swanson's Grocery Market was known for fresh local vegetables, but records also indicate that the local men liked hanging out there and talking for many hours. Here, a few men are in front, probably discussing something of high importance. (Courtesy of the Nodaway Valley Historical Museum Archives.)

This image looks west on the north side of the square. Through time, the square has been an important gathering place as well as a location to get supplies. (Courtesy of the Nodaway Valley Historical Museum Archives.)

Looking west from the corner of the north side, City Bakery can be seen. On the west side of the square is the corner where Taylor Pharmacy is located today. (Courtesy of the Nodaway Valley Historical Museum Archives.)

Built in 1866, the Linderman Hotel welcomed many travelers passing through Clarinda. It was torn down in the 1970s. (Courtesy of the Nodaway Valley Historical Museum Archives.)

Known all across the area as one of the nicest places to stay, the Linderman Hotel was especially known for its great chefs and private drivers who could take visitors anywhere they might need to go. With the invention of the automobile, the overhang was added to the building in the 1920s. (Both, courtesy of the Nodaway Valley Historical Museum Archives.)

This is a wonderful shot from the top of the courthouse looking northwest at the Linderman hotel. (Courtesy of the Nodaway Valley Historical Museum Archives.)

As in many other towns, parking meters were placed around the square to raise money for the city. It was exciting for all; this made a great photo opportunity for the local paper. (Courtesy of the Nodaway Valley Historical Museum Archives.)

One of the most famous and popular photographs of early Clarinda life, this image was taken from the south side of the square in front of the Weils store before its move to two locations on the west side of the square. Featured is a traveling family coming through town with their team of oxen. The local citizens, as well as the dogs, could not help stopping to admire the transportation. (Courtesy of the Nodaway Valley Historical Museum Archives.)

A series of photographs were taken at different times through the history of Clarinda showing the views from the courthouse at dusk. This one was captured during the holiday shopping season in 1977. The Christmas lights hanging from the courthouse building can be seen. (Courtesy of the Nodaway Valley Historical Museum Archives.)

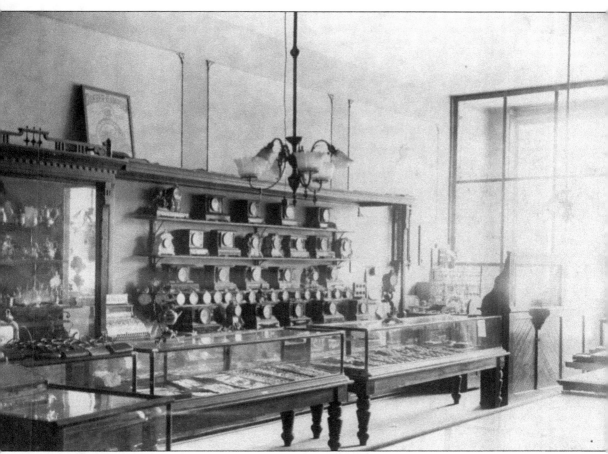

One of the glimmering stores on the south side was Pedersen's Jewelry. As soon as the building was erected in 1893 and ready for business, they had a steady flow of business. In the early days, the stock ranged from clocks to eyeglasses. Some of their silverware can still found on Clarinda tables today. (Courtesy of the Nodaway Valley Historical Museum Archives.)

Here is the north side of the square with the bank building before it was torn down. This photograph was taken in 1957 in the hopes that the north side could be updated in appearance. The image worked. Shortly after, improvements were made on four of the building fronts, including the Gamble's store next door. (Courtesy of the Nodaway Valley Historical Museum Archives.)

This image captures a community New Years celebration in 1902 in front of Pedersen's Jewelry store. (Courtesy of the Nodaway Valley Historical Museum Archives.)

The Page County Bank building was built in 1876 and used for many years. Over time, it has been used as a law firm, and a variety of local business were located in the basement. This building still stands today. The men are Charles Linderman, John Miller, and O.V. Huddle (bank teller). (Courtesy of the Nodaway Valley Historical Museum Archives.)

William Orr practiced law on the top floor of the Page County Bank building for many years. He is most remembered for his drive for new business and the gift of a public library. He made sure that Clarinda received one of the Carnegie libraries through a grant that Orr applied for on Clarinda's behalf in 1908. (Courtesy of the Nodaway Valley Historical Museum Archives.)

Featured on the cover of this book, this building still enriches the community today as a lovely antique store on the south side of the square. One can almost smell the homemade bread that was sold daily. (Courtesy of the Nodaway Valley Historical Museum Archives.)

Pictured here is the Page County Bank Building. As with most of the photographs archived at the Nodaway Valley Historical Museum, this one is undated. But, the year 1876 can be seen in relief below the peak of the building. There were many trees that lined all sides of the square. (Courtesy of the Nodaway Valley Historical Museum Archives.)

This photograph shows the view of the half block off the southeast corner of the square, begun in 1882. Business owners are busy at work, along with a few parked buggies. This block housed Clarinda's local newspaper, the *Journal* (on the corner) and Johnson Grocery (to the east). (Courtesy of the Nodaway Valley Historical Museum Archives.)

This photograph shows a men's hat sale at Friedman's Clothier. Many of these boater-style hats were sold and could be seen on a stroll around the square. (Courtesy of the Nodaway Valley Historical Museum Archives.)

Moving forward to the 1920s, pictured here is Petersons Mercantile with its lovely showcase front window. Next door, one could pick up a lovely gift at Christie's. Many of this building's cosmetic details are still visible today. (Courtesy of the Nodaway Valley Historical Museum Archives.)

This photograph was taken from one of the benches on the grounds of the Page County Courthouse. This image is one of few of the square that extends down to the grand Palace Livery Stable. This building is no longer standing, but one can almost hear the horses entering the front and exiting at the end of the building after a long day of shopping and visiting around the square. (Courtesy of the Nodaway Valley Historical Museum Archives.)

This 1977 photograph offers a view well beyond the holiday shopping going on below on Grant Street. This would have been snapped while standing in the top section of the courthouse. (Courtesy of the Nodaway Valley Historical Museum Archives.)

Popcorn Lottie was a well known face. While mothers shopped, fathers walked children around the corner by Gamble's for a warm bag of peanuts or popcorn. To this day, a photograph of Lottie is still one of the most requested at the Nodaway Valley Historical Museum. (Courtesy of the Nodaway Valley Historical Museum Archives.)

Here is a look at the southeast corner of the square. K.W. Hoar Groceries is on the corner, and there is advertising for Hobson Grocery, which was not located at this address. The *Herald Journal* moved a few times, and is still well-circulated today. (Courtesy of the Nodaway Valley Historical Museum Archives.)

This photograph taken in the 1950s provides a view of both the Farm Credit Office and Hawley Rexall Drug Store, which was one of the longest running businesses on the square. It was the only place in town during the 1950s to get Fade Proof Snap Shots. (Courtesy of the Nodaway Valley Historical Museum Archives.)

This is one of the oldest photographs of the courthouse, which was built in 1866 at a cost of $7,465. The picture was taken after 1877, when the top observation tower was added. It was a picturesque winter day; the icy treetops are especially beautiful. (Courtesy of the Nodaway Valley Historical Museum Archives.)

This is another great photograph of the beloved courthouse, taken around 1900. This building is still a symbol of arriving home for all who have lived in Page County. (Courtesy of the Nodaway Valley Historical Museum Archives.)

Although this photograph of the first official post office is undated, one can feel the pride in the new building that still stands today one block north of the square on Sixteenth Street. The number of citizens featured in the image, including the helper dog at lower left, endears it to modern viewers. (Courtesy of the Nodaway Valley Historical Museum Archives.)

In 1908, is was decided that a larger and more durable post office was needed. Pictured here in the 1940s, this building still graces the community today. (Courtesy of the Nodaway Valley Historical Museum Archives.)

Business space was needed on all four sides of the square, so the alleyways were filled in with small, narrow buildings to make room for more growth. This is a view from the south-side alley before the new filler buildings were built. Once again, this image captures one of Clarinda's four-legged friends, making its way south. Note the tower atop the courthouse showing wear from weather. It was later updated in 1950 after a fire. (Courtesy of the Nodaway Valley Historical Museum Archives.)

This empty old lot was to become the Clarinda Post Office. Pictured here the day before construction began in 1908, the scene is absent of hustle and bustle. Note the prominent advertising in the background. Dr. Pierce's advertising signs existed in many areas in the community. He had a remedy for anything that might ail, and Weil's Clothing is still in business today. (Courtesy of the Nodaway Valley Historical Museum Archives.)

Three

OFF THE SQUARE

The square was not the only place for activities, and Clarinda has many scenes to admire. Over these years of American growth and expansion, the development of the community progressed quite quickly. With the increase of Clarinda's population, there was a need to branch out from the central square, with the streets becoming longer and longer. With the expansion to accommodate people came changes to the landscape and scenery. The arrival of coal, bricks, trains, electricity, the automobile, and concrete spurred the renovation of older establishments and the building of new places of gathering and homes for families to make their own. With this growth, businesses became established on a larger scale. Some of them are still a part of the lives of Clarinda residents today. These years of growth also found Clarinda desiring to be set apart from surrounding communities. This is evident in the architecture styles that were chosen for the buildings, churches, schools, and libraries. Along with physical infrastructure, many organizations were founded at this time. Families wanted to make Clarinda into a true cultural center for Page County. The desire was to make Clarinda the place to be, not just because it was the county seat but because it was a place of culture and modern thought, providing theaters (drama and film), reading material with the first library, flowers and trees everywhere, and many churches to choose from. In this chapter, enjoy the journey of industry, entertainment, and culture in the community of Clarinda.

The northwest corner of the square was the place to find all things shiny and bright during the Clarinda Christmas season. For many years through the 1950s, the community was allowed to host the perfect tree there for all to adore. (Courtesy of the Nodaway Valley Historical Museum Archives.)

This photograph illustrates the hardships of winter travel before Clarinda enjoyed modern streets. The view from the top of West Main Street looks toward the square; note the absence of electrical wires. There is nothing but icy winter trees to block the view. The fences along the fronts of homes were used to keep the milking cows within the yards. (Courtesy of the Nodaway Valley Historical Museum Archives.)

Pictured here is Billy Ward picking up or dropping off a few patrons at the Henshaw Hotel with his brand-new carriage wagon. He was a well-known face around town, transporting many people to and from locations within the city. (Courtesy of the Nodaway Valley Historical Museum Archives.)

Here we see three dashing gentlemen admiring the weather during their stay at the Henshaw Hotel. The Henshaw Hotel was on the corner of Lincoln and Fifteenth Streets (Courtesy of the Nodaway Valley Historical Museum Archives.)

The pride of the men working at Tomlinson Harness & Saddle is apparent. This business tended to the needs of an important mode of transportation of the day—the horse. The shop was located at two different places in Clarinda, on East Main Street and East Water Street. (Courtesy of the Nodaway Valley Historical Museum Archives.)

This photograph was taken on South Sixteenth Street near Richardson Lumber just off Water Street during a heavy rainstorm. Note the little boy observing the flooding waters. (Courtesy of the Nodaway Valley Historical Museum Archives.)

This sunny photograph was taken during the 1920s. This impressive building was built in 1908 as the Carnegie Library, thanks to a grant from Andrew Carnegie. Today the citizens of Southwest Iowa enjoy it as the newly restored Clarinda Carnegie Art Museum. (Courtesy of the Nodaway Valley Historical Museum Archives.)

Pictured here is A.W. Drake and Sons, dealers in farm implements. The location of this business is unknown. Drake supplied all of Southwest Iowa with the equipment that was needed to prosper. The men are posing with some examples of the latest in farming implements used in the area. (Courtesy of the Nodaway Valley Historical Museum Archives.)

This building is just one of the many grand business structures built off the Clarinda Square. William Henry Harnagel was born in 1874, the first son to a German-born father. Harnagel erected this building in 1910, and it served the south of town well as a market and was handed down to several owners, including William E. Sims and then his son Boyd Sims during the 1940s. (Courtesy of the Nodaway Valley Historical Museum Archives.)

Here is an expansive view of the Nodaway River looking south. This is one of many photographs housed at the Nodaway Valley Museum that curators know little about. (Courtesy of the Nodaway Valley Historical Museum Archives.)

1910 LEE LITE PLANT

The Lee Lite Power Plant was one block north of the square on Fifteenth Street. Note the brick streets, which were paved in 1902, and the new power poles ready to distribute electricity throughout the town. (Courtesy of the Nodaway Valley Historical Museum Archives.)

Horse-drawn carriages created the need for a variety of supplemental businesses. Clarinda Carriage Works took pride in their ability to keep everyone's rigs in top-notch condition. This photograph was taken in 1880, when the wooden sidewalks were still present. (Courtesy of the Nodaway Valley Historical Museum Archives.)

In 1921, the Clarinda Country Club was built. These grounds are still enjoyed today, although several new buildings have been added. (Courtesy of the Nodaway Valley Historical Museum Archives.)

With the arrival of the steam engine, many more visitors came to Clarinda. Many excited passengers rode the rails to arrive at the depot at the south end of town. (Courtesy of the Nodaway Valley Historical Museum Archives.)

The place to be on a hot summer day was the American Legion Post 98 pool, built in 1927. This outdoor pool was replaced by an innovative dome-style pool in the 1980s just across East Washington Street. (Courtesy of the Nodaway Valley Historical Museum Archives.)

The Dairy Sweet was located at Seventh and Washington Streets during the 1950s and 1960s. For 15¢, one could get a sundae; with a little more jingle in one's pocket, 25¢ would buy a chocolate shake. Courtesy of the Nodaway Valley Historical Museum Archives.)

This is one of the photographs at the Nodaway Valley Historical Museum that has been enhanced. The City Mill was located at Fourteenth and Chestnut Streets. Many loaves of bread were baked, in part, because of this mill. (Courtesy of the Nodaway Valley Historical Museum Archives.)

Pictured here is Fairyland, a favorite summertime haunt just northwest of town. This special area is known for its fireflies during warm weather. (Courtesy of the Nodaway Valley Historical Museum Archives.)

A street-paving crew pauses for a picture while working their way through Clarinda in the fall of 1913. The original bricks were placed in 1902 and later replaced with concrete over the course of many years. (Courtesy of the Nodaway Valley Historical Museum Archives.)

Evans used-automobile dealer was located behind the present-day post office. Notice the handy phone booth placed just were one might need to make a call. (Courtesy of the Nodaway Valley Historical Museum Archives.)

Here is the inside of Evans auto showroom around 1946. One could browse through this selection of used cars to find the perfect fit. (Courtesy of the Nodaway Valley Historical Museum Archives.)

Lisle Manufacturing was established in 1903 by Charles Albert Lisle. This company grew with the development of the industrial world to withstand the test of time. Clarinda has been fortunate to share in the celebration of over 110 years of success. Now the company offers more than 400 automotive tools and related items. (Courtesy of the Nodaway Valley Historical Museum Archives.)

Charles Albert Lisle was the founder of Lisle Manufacturing. During the 1920s, the company entered the automotive market when it began producing master ignition vibrators for the Ford Model T. The company today is managed by the fourth generation of the Lisle family. (Courtesy of the Nodaway Valley Historical Museum Archives.)

Lisle Manufacturing originally made horse-powered well-drilling machines. The company soon expanded its offerings to include washing machines, cream separators, and reel lawn mowers. (Courtesy of the Nodaway Valley Historical Museum Archives.)

The Clarinda Lawn Mower Company, which employed over 20 men and an office staff, produced over 40 mowers per day. The local paper reported that orders arrived daily from all over the country. (Courtesy of the Nodaway Valley Historical Museum Archives.)

This is one of the finest pieces of advertising from the Clarinda Lawn Mowing Company. Here local resident Mrs. Armstrong and her lovely daughter pose, apparently to show that even ladies could use the new mower device. (Courtesy of the Nodaway Valley Historical Museum Archives.)

This lovely lady, identified only as Charlotte, was also used to advertise lawn mowers. On the back, it states once again how easy a Clarinda Lawn Mowing Company lawn mower is to use. (Courtesy of the Nodaway Valley Historical Museum Archives.)

Mrs. Bracken, a local businesswoman, was glad to help out with advertising as well. (Courtesy of the Nodaway Valley Historical Museum Archives.)

This Clarinda Lawn Mowing Company advertisement featured raised areas for added texture. (Courtesy of the Nodaway Valley Historical Museum Archives.)

Here is another great example of progress. The railroad was expanded to reach the east side of what would become Lisle Manufacturing Company. In the background, the Shambaugh Mill is visible. Clarinda was served by railroads from five different directions. (Courtesy of the Nodaway Valley Historical Museum Archives.)

The Page County Jail was built just off the corner of Lincoln and Fifteenth Streets. Much about the location has changed, but the original white concrete building has been updated and is still used today. (Courtesy of the Nodaway Valley Historical Museum Archives.)

The Pearson Coal Mine was located to the west outside Clarinda. The miners are pictured here on a break, with wagons ready to deliver more coal to Clarinda residents. (Courtesy of the Nodaway Valley Historical Museum Archives.)

This railroad led right into the Pearson Mine so that the company might transport coal to all areas of Southwest Iowa. (Courtesy of the Nodaway Valley Historical Museum Archives.)

American Railway Express was established by the US Railway Administration in 1918 as part of the federal government's takeover of the country's rail system as a safety precaution during World War I. This is an exemplary photograph of the local brick streets as well. (Courtesy of the Nodaway Valley Historical Museum Archives.)

Iowa State Hospital for the Insane was built in 1884. It was the third asylum in the state of Iowa and remains in operation today. This is an idyllic view through the trees on the Iowa State Hospital grounds (currently known as the Clarinda Treatment Complex) looking toward Hope Hall. (Courtesy of the Nodaway Valley Historical Museum Archives.)

Berry's Seed Company, a mail-order seed-distribution business, was founded in 1885 in Clarinda by A.A. Berry. Berry's Seed Company grew into retail stores in the 1950s. (Courtesy of the Nodaway Valley Historical Museum Archives.)

All of the Berry's Seed Company employees gathered for this group portrait outside the mail-order office. This location was one block west of the square on Washington Street. Today, some of the old advertising on the side of the brick building is still visible. (Courtesy of the Nodaway Valley Historical Museum Archives.)

The Shambaugh Mill, located behind Lisle Manufacturing, served the local residents well for many years.

Four

OUR SCHOOLS

Clarinda residents have always taken great pride in their school systems. One of the first things established in Clarinda was a place for education. A little shack built on the south side of the square stood for all that was important for the people who settled this area. Later, an entire city block at Grant and Fifteenth Streets was designated for the perpetual use of education, called the school block.

This chapter is dedicated to the many people who sought out an education. No matter the distance, the weather, or other difficulties, they sought it out, and they found it. Always present in the Clarinda community was the desire to be more advanced, to grow, and to share that knowledge with others, and this included the youth. Over the many years since the establishment of the school block, many children have grown, learned, and left through the doors of myriad buildings that stood on that same block. The author attended school on this block for three years of her education. The structure was as grand and embracing as the education.

Clarinda's eighth grade graduating class of 1916 is pictured here. (Courtesy of the Nodaway Valley Historical Museum Archives.)

The first Lincoln School at Lincoln and 19th Streets burned in 1920 and was rebuilt and named the new Lincoln School.

North Ward School, a wonderful piece of architecture, was sadly torn down in 1956. It was replaced with the school that was built as a tribute to President McKinley. McKinley School was used for elementary classes from 1956 to 1998 but is now used as a district school office for the Clarinda School Systems. (Courtesy of the Nodaway Valley Historical Museum Archives.)

Many students know this as the "Old South Building." This was the original schoolhouse located at Grant and Thirteenth Streets, adjacent to the Promenade. This school was built in 1877 and served all children of the area. This site was also the location of a speech given by Pres. Theodore Roosevelt in 1903. Many gathered there that day and leaned out all of the windows for a glimpse of the president, who was only in Clarinda for 30 minutes or so. (Courtesy of the Nodaway Valley Historical Museum Archives.)

The Clarinda Educational Institute was located on West Clark Street. It was an invaluable tool to prepare the youth for a possible college education. Sadly, it was destroyed by a fire in 1924. (Courtesy of the Nodaway Valley Historical Museum Archives.)

This poor photograph is the only image in existence of the first official Clarinda High School built on the school block. This photograph, taken in 1876, captures the school at the end of its life, before the completion of the Old South School just a few short blocks away. (Courtesy of the Nodaway Valley Historical Museum Archives.)

In 1912, the new Clarinda High School opened. It was built to accommodate the growing number of local students in Page County. It served for higher education until 1922.

In 1922, the school block was once again updated with this new larger building, known simply as Clarinda High School. This building served the children of Clarinda from 1923 to 1968 as a high school and then as a junior high school. It has been torn down and replaced with the beautiful Lied Library. (Courtesy of the Nodaway Valley Historical Museum Archives.)

This school served the children of Clarinda from 1912 to 1922. It was also merely known as Clarinda High School. (Courtesy of the Nodaway Valley Historical Museum Archives.)

West Building was located at the corner of Twentieth and Lincoln Streets. It served as the high school for Clarinda from 1905 to 1912 and then as an elementary school until it burned in 1921. (Courtesy of the Nodaway Valley Historical Museum Archives.)

This was the new school that was built in the West Building location after the fire. It was to be called Lincoln School, in honor of Pres. Abraham Lincoln. In 1921, it cost $18,000 to build. This school served as an elementary school up until 1990, when it was closed and then later torn down. (Courtesy of the Nodaway Valley Historical Museum Archives.)

Five

HOMES, PROMENADES, AND PEOPLE

Over the years of Clarinda's history, there have been many remarkable people who have called it home. With that comes amazing structures and home design from each of those times. This chapter is dedicated to those structures in the community that locals pass by every day and wonder about. There is not a book large enough to dedicate the proper amount of details and information about the amazing souls who grew and helped Clarinda grow over the last 160-plus years. Clarinda is and was home to people of spirit and brilliance, along with quite a few characters. But along the way, homes were built, and the town evolved. Through that journey, photographs were taken, not of every single thing or event or person, but many. Many of those are housed for safekeeping at the Nodaway Valley Historical Museum. Every day, curators are delighted to receive more and perhaps uncover one or link some together through families both old and new.

This home was built by the husband of 4-H founder Jessie Field Shambaugh. Located at 401 North Eighteenth Street of the Promenade at the top of Lincoln Street, it is a lovely traditional brick Colonial. (Courtesy of the Nodaway Valley Historical Museum Archives.)

This home at the top of Main Street has been admired by many high schoolers on their way to school every morning. It was built by Forest Davidson in 1896. (Courtesy of the Nodaway Valley Historical Museum Archives.)

This home, located on North Fifteenth and State Streets, was the family residence of Alfred Victor Hunt, a local mercantile businessman on the square during the late 1800s. (Courtesy of the Nodaway Valley Historical Museum Archives.)

This sweeping panoramic photograph was taken at the turn of the 20th century looking north at the corner of Washington and Seventeenth Streets. (Courtesy of the Nodaway Valley Historical Museum Archives.)

This panorama looking west on the corner of State and Eighteenth Streets captures a glimpse of what was the Powers Hospital (left) with a multigenerational home (next on the right). The home at far right was torn down during the 1920s to make way for smaller residences. (Courtesy of the Nodaway Valley Historical Museum Archives.)

Jay Squires, the violin maker, called this home for many years. Today this is known as the 300 block of East Main Street. (Courtesy of the Nodaway Valley Historical Museum Archives.)

This photograph was taken in the late 1800s by the proud Mr. Friedman. In the background is his brand-new home on the 500 block of North Fifteenth Street. In the foreground is his smiling wife and shiny buggy. Even the horse is posing. Friedman owned a clothing mercantile on the square for many years. (Courtesy of the Nodaway Valley Historical Museum Archives.)

The Hawley home sadly was torn down at the beginning of the 1900s, but what a magnificent house it was in its glory years. The Hawley family built and owned this home for three generations. It was located on the 300 block of Eighteenth Street. When it was torn down, there was enough room to accommodate three new houses. (Courtesy of the Nodaway Valley Historical Museum Archives.)

The historic home of Col. William Peters Hepburn is on the northeast corner of Lincoln and Nineteenth Streets. At one time, this was the only home on the entire block. Later, lots were sold off to build other homes. Now, the block is home to four families. (Courtesy of the Nodaway Valley Historical Museum Archives.)

Known to many generations as Killingsworth Hospital, this was actually built as a home by N.B. Moore, Page County's first millionaire. Later, he sold the building to the City of Clarinda for $100 to be used as a hospital. This building stood at the corner of Chestnut and Eighteenth Streets along the Promenade. (Courtesy of the Nodaway Valley Historical Museum Archives.)

This home is one that many still enjoy on their nightly walks around the Boulevard, or as it used to be called, the Promenade. It is located on the corner of Eighteenth and Chestnut Streets, opposite the corner location of Killingsworth Hospital. Today, it is quite a sight at Christmastime, as it is specially decorated for the season. (Courtesy of the Nodaway Valley Historical Museum Archives.)

Located at Seventeenth and Washington Streets, this imposing house was known as the Thompson home. Thompson was a local lawyer with an office on the square that was sadly demolished in the mid-1900s. (Courtesy of the Nodaway Valley Historical Museum Archives.)

This view of the Clarinda Promenade is looking north from the top of the hill at Grant Street. From the clean concrete streets and the new car, it is likely this photograph was taken between 1908 and 1912. (Courtesy of the Nodaway Valley Historical Museum Archives.)

Although, this photograph is in poor shape, it is one of the only views of the original dirt streets. This image was captured while standing at Nishna and Sixteenth Streets looking south in the winter. Note the thawed snow off to the left. (Courtesy of the Nodaway Valley Historical Museum Archives.)

Clarinda was just one of many communities in the area that hosted Chautauqua adult-education events in the United States. In Clarinda, the event would last for many days, with people actually camping out on the park grounds. (Courtesy of the Nodaway Valley Historical Museum Archives.)

Here is a great shot taken by a visitor of a gentleman passing by the Henshaw Hotel. This image is looking north on Fifteenth Street and shows all four corners of Fifteenth Street and Lincoln Boulevard. It is amazing how many trees were growing strong at this intersection. (Courtesy of the Nodaway Valley Historical Museum Archives.)

This photograph has been enhanced to show further details of the street scene on the west side of the square during an evening of lights in 1890. (Courtesy of the Nodaway Valley Historical Museum Archives.)

The porch of the Walker home on the Boulevard at 300 West Main Street is pictured here in wintertime. Walker operated the funeral home in Clarinda for many years. Note the ice hanging as if placed for the holidays. (Courtesy of the Nodaway Valley Historical Museum Archives.)

This is another shot from the top of the hill on south Eighteenth Street looking north. It would have been at the end of summer when all things are in bloom. (Courtesy of the Nodaway Valley Historical Museum Archives.)

One of Clarinda's favorite streets is West Willow. At the end of this lamp-lit boulevard sits the historic home built by Berry Seed Company founder Andrew Berry in 1913 to showcase his success in business. (Courtesy of the Nodaway Valley Historical Museum Archives.)

Residence of J. P. Kenea, corner Eighteenth and Grant streets, Clarinda, Iowa.

This was the location that the Kenea family called home from the late 1800s to the 1920s. J.P. Kenea owned the local *Herald* newspaper while assisted by his college-educated wife who was known for exploring the town for news to report. This house still stands today at the top of Eighteenth and Grant Streets. (Courtesy of the Nodaway Valley Historical Museum Archives.)

Six

OUR SOLDIERS

During more than 160 years, Clarinda patriots stood tall when the call was given for help in times of slavery and segregation and to fight and assist other nations around the world. During the Civil War, men, with the support of their ladies, stood to such a call with a mighty force. Page County was given the distinguished honor of the being the Banner County of Iowa. The community had more boys and men per capita volunteer for the Civil War than any other county in Iowa. Clarinda was awarded a flag for this honor. It was housed and kept at the local courthouse for many years after the war. This chapter is dedicated to those who served Clarinda and Page County with honor. Sadly, only so much room can be allowed, so many are not present on these pages. Information on all who have served has been complied and is housed at the Nodaway Valley Historical Museum for all citizens to learn of and honor all of the men, women, and boys from Clarinda who served the country. Included are the accounts of two special soldiers. William Pinckney Buchanan was a dragoon soldier with the 6th US Infantry. This young soldier was serving the government by scouting the land of the future state of Iowa. He drowned in a local river and was buried on-site with his horse; in May 1904, he was removed and now lays at rest in Arlington National Cemetery. Daniel Dow was a messenger boy during the Revolutionary War who later traveled west and settled here in Page County for much of his adult life. Dow was laid to rest on February 7, 1860, at the local Grove County Cemetery with Daughters of the American Revolution markers to let all know of his early service. To all of the local men and women who served the country, thank you.

This image bears the simple identification "Parade on Memorial Day." (Courtesy of the Nodaway Valley Historical Museum Archives.)

Clarinda commissioned and dedicated a Civil War monument like so many communities across the country. It was reported that almost all the citizens of the town and county showed up for the dedication in 1913. The Soldiers' Monument on the courthouse square was paid for by public subscription to show respect for the men who fought in the war. (Courtesy of the Nodaway Valley Historical Museum Archives.)

Civil War Congressional Medal of Honor winner Richard Morgan poses with his family. In a single engagement near Columbus, Georgia, on April 16, 1865, five members of the 4th Iowa Cavalry and two members of the 3rd Iowa Cavalry captured the battle flags of their opponents. Each of these seven men, all from the state of Iowa, received Medals of Honor. Corporal Morgan of Company A, 4th Iowa Cavalry, was cited for entering the enemy's works, where he "contested" with the bearer of the enemy flag for its possession. Richard Morgan worked as a guard at the Fort Madison penitentiary before he returned to the Taylor/Page County area. (Courtesy of the Nodaway Valley Historical Museum Archives.)

Civil War brevet brigadier general (Union), US senator, and Idaho governor; all of these describe Thomas Bowen. At the outbreak of the Civil War, Bowen was a lawyer in practice in Clarinda when commissioned as a captain in the 13th Kansas Volunteer Infantry. Promoted to colonel in 1863, he commanded a brigade with the 7th Army Corps for the entire frontier campaign. For his military service, he was brevetted brigadier general of US volunteers in 1865. After the war, he settled in Arkansas and was a justice of the Supreme Court of Arkansas from 1867 to 1871. In 1871, he was appointed governor of the Idaho Territory by Pres. Ulysses S. Grant, where he served until 1875. He relocated to Colorado in 1876, was elected judge of the Fourth Judicial District (serving until 1880), and served as a member of the Colorado House of Representatives in 1882 and 1883. He was elected as a Republican to the US Senate and served until 1889. (Courtesy of the Nodaway Valley Historical Museum Archives.)

Dr. Powers served during the Civil War, after which he returned to Clarinda and remained in practice until his death in 1929. He also served as assistant superintendent of the Clarinda State Hospital for the Insane from 1891 until 1893. (Courtesy of the Nodaway Valley Historical Museum Archives.)

Pictured here is one of Clarinda's finest and most beloved teachers, Charles Arnold. Prior to his teaching career, Arnold was a soldier during the Spanish-American War. When the war with Spain broke out in 1897, he proved his patriotism by serving with Company M of the 51st Iowa as a private soldier. Returning home with fever from the war, he never regained his health and passed away at the age of 41. (Courtesy of the Nodaway Valley Historical Museum Archives.)

Frozen in time in this image is the day that over 2,000 people attended the military funeral of the Cooper brothers, Lawrence and John D. "Delbert," sons of John and Martha Jane Cooper. The brothers were honored in the courthouse yard in Clarinda. It must have been the most attended funeral of any ever held in this city. The two caskets of the boys who gave up their lives in France for their country were side by side, resting on supports on the walk in front of the north steps of the courthouse. (Courtesy of the Nodaway Valley Historical Museum Archives.)

Pictured here is Delbert Cooper. The boys went from Clarinda with the Company F boys to Villisca, then to Des Moines for training and overseas as members of the 168th Infantry, 42nd (Rainbow) Division. Lawrence met his death at the Battle of Chateau Thierry on August 27, 1918. John D. Cooper, or Delbert as he was known, was a member of the 32nd Division machine gun battalion and was killed just a month later than his brother on September 27, 1918. (Courtesy of the Nodaway Valley Historical Museum Archives.)

One of Clarinda's most beloved was Ernest Tomlinson. This young man served as a sergeant in the Army Air Force during World War II. He was killed in action in 1944. (Courtesy of the Nodaway Valley Historical Museum Archives.)

Fred Brummett was "a young man of splendid character," according to *The Price of our Heritage* by Winifred E. Robb. Brummett was wounded in action on March 9, 1918, at Neu Ville, and died in the hospital at Baccarat on March 10, 1918. He was buried on March 13 in grave No. 24 in Baccarat Cemetery. He was the son of Rushia Brummett of Clarinda, Iowa. Private Brummett was wounded in the back by a high-explosive shell. He immediately received the best of care from American and French surgeons, but they failed to save him. His last words were about his mother, who he loved very much. Private Brummett was awarded the Croix de Guerre before he died. (Courtesy of the Nodaway Valley Historical Museum Archives.)

Clarinda High School 1938 graduate Vernon J. Baker was a US Army officer who received the Medal of Honor, the highest military award given by the government for his valorous actions during World War II on April 5–6, 1945, near Viareggio, Italy. Baker was the only living black American World War II veteran of the seven who were belatedly awarded the Medal of Honor when it was bestowed upon him by Pres. Bill Clinton in 1997. At the time he left the military in 1968, he was a first lieutenant. Baker died in 2010 at the age of 90 and is buried at Arlington Cemetery. (Courtesy of the Nodaway Valley Historical Museum Archives.)

This photograph is truly a masterpiece. The photographer who captured this cold winter night from the top of the courthouse looking northwest is unknown. The Linderman Hotel is visible in the background, along with many other businesses around the square. The Page County Veterans Arch was finalized on May 31, 1945. The arch still stands today and confirms Clarinda and Page County's dedication and support for their veterans. (Courtesy of the Nodaway Valley Historical Museum Archives.)

On October 7, 1945, the last Japanese prisoner left the Clarinda Prisoner of War camp. This photograph captures that moment. The Clarinda POW camp, built in 1943, housed German, Italian, and Japanese prisoners. (Courtesy of the Nodaway Valley Historical Museum Archives.)

Frank Barr is pictured here in his World War I uniform. He returned home, passed away in Clarinda on October 9, 1976, and was buried at the Clarinda Cemetery. (Courtesy of the Nodaway Valley Historical Museum Archives.)

A common sight during World War I and World War II, residents are bidding goodbye as the young men head off to fight for their country. Here Eldon Good is saying goodbye to family members. (Courtesy of the Nodaway Valley Historical Museum Archives.)

This is a great view from a distance of Camp Clarinda, which was located at the site of the present-day Clarinda Airport. From 1943 to 1945, the camp housed over 3,000 prisoners. Many of the structures still exist within the community after being purchased at a sale after the camp closed in 1945.

This is the historic Page County Veterans Arch. These unidentified soldiers are celebrating during the annual Memorial Day remembrance. (Courtesy of the Nodaway Valley Historical Museum Archives.)

Seven

FROM THE AIR

Over the years, many citizens have taken to the air during all seasons to record the growth and glory of the town. This chapter is dedicated to those aerial images. The heart of the town has always been the square. This has been the place to gather over the years and where to go for information or advice. The center of town always had what one needed, whether that was groceries, a new dress or hat, or a good conversation on current events. Everything that Clarinda has done to grow and expand came from this center of the community. Many of the structures in these photographs are no longer, having vanished into the past.

Pictured here is the fence around the courthouse, which does not exist today. Also visible is the Civil War monument, on the southwest corner, which was erected in 1917. (Courtesy of the Nodaway Valley Historical Museum Archives.)

Looking northwest from the courthouse, the Linderman Hotel can be seen, along with many homes farther out. In the background, note the original Lincoln School before it burned in 1921. (Courtesy of the Nodaway Valley Historical Museum Archives.)

This shot captures a great view of the courthouse and its surroundings. The number of trees is astounding. (Courtesy of the Nodaway Valley Historical Museum Archives.)

In 1908, an unknown person took it upon themselves to photograph Clarinda from all sides of the courthouse. This image, looking north, provides a glimpse of the streets and homes of the time. (Courtesy of the Nodaway Valley Historical Museum Archives.)

Pictured here is the west side of the Linderman Hotel. In the distance is Killingsworth Hospital. Several of the homes on the right are still standing today. (Courtesy of the Nodaway Valley Historical Museum Archives.)

This is the only known photograph that captures the view to the northeast from the Clarinda Courthouse. Behind is the Lee Power Plant, along with many homes. It looks pretty busy at Kelly's Tires on the corner. (Courtesy of the Nodaway Valley Historical Museum Archives.)

Taken in 1902, this view looking southeast from the courthouse is marvelous. It is the only photograph in existence of the Palace Livery Stable. It also features Lisle Manufacturing and the Swift building in the background. (Courtesy of the Nodaway Valley Historical Museum Archives.)

Looking southwest from the courthouse in 1902 is the Richardson Lumber Yard, which sadly does not exist today. But many of the homes pictured still stand, including the one on the left with the black trim. (Courtesy of the Nodaway Valley Historical Museum Archives.)

Pictured here is a very brave man atop the Clarinda Water Tower. Although it is not in the best of shape, what a great story it tells. (Courtesy of the Nodaway Valley Historical Museum Archives.)

Eight

JUST FOR FUN

This last chapter is dedicated to the Clarinda citizens' spirit, humor, and general love of life. It was not just a few citizens of the past or a certain section of society that built Clarinda's history, it was all people. Clarinda's citizens have always been its greatest asset. Their knowledge, creativity, and hard work enabled growth and prosperity as all citizens banded together, learned from each other, and moved on with the changes going on all around them over the years. Housed at the Nodaway Valley Historical Museum are many wedding, prom, party, and christening outfits within the textile collection. These items showcase the spirit that is still present today. Locals continue to battle in the world and suffer with sadness and loss, yet time and time again, Clarinda residents rise to the occasion and band together to assist, fix, restore, and serve the city. This strength rises from a love of life, good times, and laughter.

Anthony Loranz's family was born in Germany. After arriving in Clarinda, they became one of the leading families during the 1800s. The Loranz Company stood on the south side of the square for many years and served Clarinda for all documents, titles, and abstracts. Loranz's descendants continued on for many years, with Carrie Loranz publishing her family's accounts of the early beginnings of Clarinda. (Courtesy of the Nodaway Valley Historical Museum Archives.)

The wedding of Adolph Sunderman and Rosey Hennemen in 1912 brought joy and celebration to all in the community. This wedding dress is one of many housed with care at the Nodaway Valley Historical Museum. (Courtesy of the Nodaway Valley Historical Museum Archives.)

"The unknown sewing ladies" is what the curators at Nodaway Valley Historical Museum call these ladies. (Courtesy of the Nodaway Valley Historical Museum Archives.)

In 1892, a special party was held at the home of Mary Sayer Richardson. This was in celebration of the leap year; note the white powdered wigs. At that time, invitations were handwritten and delivered. On average, there were at least three parties per week reported in the local newspaper. (Courtesy of the Nodaway Valley Historical Museum Archives.)

Here is a citizen of spirit. Melchor Ferris traveled the United States with his program on how one can do anything with the right sense of self. Ferris lost his hands in an electrical accident in 1913. (Courtesy of the Nodaway Valley Historical Museum Archives.)

These two unidentified young gents are ready to go on the doorstep of the local newspaper the *Democrat*, which was located on the southeast corner of the square. (Courtesy of the Nodaway Valley Historical Museum Archives.)

Here, Clarinda's finest ladies are sporting the latest hat fashions. Their getups make one wonder where they were going.

The Rooster Club was a local gentlemen's club that had monthly meetings to discuss worldly happenings and local events. (Courtesy of the Nodaway Valley Historical Museum Archives.)

In the background is the Carnegie Library, which has now become the Clarinda Carnegie Art Museum. Known as Glenn Miller Avenue, this street is still one of the busiest in Clarinda. (Courtesy of the Nodaway Valley Historical Museum Archives.)

Family dinners on Sunday after church are still are a common occurrence here. (Courtesy of the Nodaway Valley Historical Museum Archives.)

This wonderful photograph shows the strength of family. (Courtesy of the Nodaway Valley Historical Museum Archives.)

Pictured here is one of the local homes decorated at Christmastime. The Butler family home was always the center of festivities over the holiday for local parties. (Courtesy of the Nodaway Valley Historical Museum Archives.)

Owner of the *Herald Journal*, Carl C. Caswell was even more known for his cartoons that often depicted current political issues of the day. (Courtesy of the Nodaway Valley Historical Museum Archives.)

Opening during the 1970s, Clarinda's dome pool was one of the first establishments in the area to look at solar power as a resource for energy. In the early 1900s, the location served as the county Chautauqua center. (Courtesy of the Nodaway Valley Historical Museum Archives.)

Children and adults alike from the local area enjoy many hours of fun at Grimes Roller Rink, which operated from 1935 to 1968. There are still many skates hiding out in home attics that could tell tales from Grimes. (Courtesy of the Nodaway Valley Historical Museum Archives.)

Rudolph Frederick Handorf came to America in 1853 from Germany. The Nodaway Valley Historical Museum can trace many current families in the area back to Handorf. (Courtesy of the Nodaway Valley Historical Museum Archives.)

This shot showcases some of the top-of-the-line business equipment that kept the Berry Seed company employing Clarinda citizens for over 75 years. (Courtesy of the Nodaway Valley Historical Museum Archives.)

The wedding of Harry and Lillie Lagerquist on February 16, 1910, was attended by many. Lillie's is one of many wedding gowns housed at the Nodaway Valley Historical Museum. (Courtesy of the Nodaway Valley Historical Museum Archives.)

Pictured here in 1926 is a May Day celebration. This annual event always ended with a flowered court of locals receiving the honors for the day. (Courtesy of the Nodaway Valley Historical Museum Archives.)

Pictured here are the State Hospital for the Insane grounds at the height of winter. The facility closed in 2015 after serving the needs of patients for over 125 years. (Courtesy of the Nodaway Valley Historical Museum Archives.)

Charles and Mamie Phillips were local residents who loved the camera and all that it could capture. This photograph was taken in Moline, Illinois, by Harrington Photography. They would often travel out of the area for that perfect new shot. (Courtesy of the Nodaway Valley Historical Museum Archives.)

Lisle Manufacturing employees often spent their lunch hour at Mrs. Preoo's Restaurant. Pictured here are a few of the young lady employees after a meal that cost 25¢. (Courtesy of the Nodaway Valley Historical Museum Archives.)

In 1942, William G. Dunn received the Army-Navy Award on behalf of Parris-Dunn Corporation for high achievement in the production of training rifles for the military.

Visit us at
arcadiapublishing.com

CPSIA information can be obtained
at www.ICGtesting.com
Printed in the USA
BVHW051330020321
601493BV00015B/1328